MW00909323

THE HOUSE THAT JACK BUILT

Author Jamila Latham
Edited by Shellih El

The House that Jack Built

The House that Jack Built

The House that Jack Built

From the Author's heart

I understand that not all that suffer with mental illness have a supportive network. So, I say be resilient in getting one. A healthy network, team, relatives, competent professionals are a huge part of the puzzle. Mental illness will make you feel like you have to do it alone, that no one understands your struggle because it is unique, and that help is limited. If you suffer from depression, bipolar disorder, anxiety, or something other that can't be located in the DSM yet, seek help as if your life depends on it, because it does. There are millions of others that have suffered and have started the Path to Recovery. You are not alone. The struggle is real, but the recovering journey is a reality as well. Although, there is no complete cure for mental health related issues, start the process in recovery, which is a very tangible road. This might mean you have to adapt some new ideas; you might have to admit that you are wrong, and others are right in some areas, and you might also have to go back in history and talk about family dynamics like I have in this book. But, I ask you to never give up fighting. We are depending on you to represent us in a way that only you can. All that makes you up to be you, is needed in the fabric of society. We need you to show up and to speak up. I believe in you.

Those that feel like they are on the verge of "losing it" this book is for you. My transparency about my struggle opened up conversations with others, that they too can become vulnerable and transparent. I share with you my recovery tools that I needed to take charge of my mental health, which everyone can use. That is the good part. These are tools that I learned along my journey of recovery that I use

The House that Jack Built

to keep me sane in an internal world that wants to tear me apart. These tools that could help anyone manage their mental health. Be proactive.

Those that have a love one that is struggling- keep holding onto hope. Sometimes your hope is the only hope that is present, because they may be depleted of all hope.
Continue to be a listening ear, while you manage your own mental health. The value of a supportive community, I can't begin stress how important it is. Your love is appreciated, and your work is valued.

The struggle is real, but so is Recovery.

The House that Jack Built

The House that Jack Built

Acknowledgment

I would like to thank the team of women that have and still surrounds me in my Discovery process. They have been loving conduits in my growth as a child of God, as a woman, as an African American woman, as a positive active member of society, and as spokesperson for those that have a Mental Illness Diagnosis. Words are not enough retribution for the spontaneous phone calls in the middle of the day, your perseverance to my strong-minded resistance to your care, and patience to my dismissiveness to your wisdom. You have taught in either word or deeds. With your help I have found my own norms. I have found my own distinctive voice. I am a better human being because of how God has graced you throughout my life.

Today, when I look in the mirror I am proud. My diagnosis does not determine my true identity, nor does my history. We all are made up of complied circumstance in our lives, but we are made up of much more. All of us have stardust in us. You might not see it, but hopefully deep within you feel it. This evolution would not have been made possible if it was not for my network of family, and friends that have held hope for me when I did not see the end to the yellow brick road.

To my Father and Mother, thank you for all that you done and continue to do.

The House that Jack Built

Table of contents

The House that Jack Built

The House that Jack Built

According to the National Association for Mental Health there are approximately 1 in 5 adults in the U.S.—43.8 million, or 18.5%—experience mental illness in a given year.
(https://www.nami.org/Learn-More/Mental-Health-By-the-Numbers, Retrieved on Jan. 8, 2018)

The House that Jack Built

Um hum she died that night, may her soul rest in peace
You know she was always looking for something
The nerve, chasing rainbows in an alleyway
You know I could still hear her scream, free me from these chains
Well Masta said we were free to go, but poor thing was chained to despair
They say she died from a broken heart, life not that hard
They trespassed on her virginity when she was twelve, too many issues on her shelves
Fighting the rain, that is God's choice you know the flowers aren't going to feed themselves.
She wanted to steal that pot of gold
Thought she was entitled
Why? Because she was born.
Even from her mother's womb she chanted liberty
Expecting a resurrection, who she thinks she is, Lazarus?
No, I heard it was more like a caterpillar to a butterfly
Oh how she wanted her name in the sky
They tried to convince her she had no right to a piece of the American pie
And for 3 nights her mother cried
Although she lives, she is still waiting to be alive.

CHAPTER ONE

The House that Jack Built

The House that Jack Built

Pulling up Rotten Roots

I was brought up in the West Oak Lane section of Philadelphia. I remember my uncle telling me how much the neighborhood has changed from the time that he grew up. When he arrived to West Oak Lane from West Philly, there were only white folks that lived in the apartment buildings surrounding the only 2 houses on the block. My great-grandparents were 1 of the only 2 home owners on the block. That was doing good for black people back in the day, however how they paid for the home has its own story. We often call that house, The House that Jack Built. My great grandfather's name was Jack, and this is the house that he built, this was his legacy. But it wasn't just the house that they built. It was the house that my great great-grandparents built and so on. It was the house that slaves built, and their slave masters built. It was the house that the traditions from down south built. Some would say it is the house that Adam and Eve built after Adam bit into the apple.

The House that Jack Built

The DNA of my grandparents showed itself up in each generation. Even if it had been someone trying to run so far from them and their "legacy", that they ran as fast as they could in the complete opposite direction. Unfortunately, masking their anger with jokes as to how bad it was growing up in this lineage. Our past always shows up eventually. Especially, if we have not dealt with it. To this day, I will often say that it's just the 1803 in me. As a kid, I remember my great grandmother being sweet and compassionate. I remember when I was very young meeting a homeless woman on the street and asked her why she didn't have a place to live. Her response was "I just don't", so I told her she can live with us. Surely, that same day she was another member of our household. Another member to add to the 12 people (on some occasions 15 people) of our household in a 4 bedroom house. Eventually, I realized how well she would fit in by her dysfunction. Lets just say she got too comfortable with the men in my house. All the young men in our household. Eventually she was gone, and so was my TV. Yes, at age 7 I had my own TV. My mom sent it to me, so I wouldn't have to choose between my cartoons or The A Team. On Saturdays, I watched wrestling with *** **** after he made me the best fried potatoes ever. Until this day I remember the recipe. I carefully watched him make them. I often studied people as a child, not only for what to do, but for what not to do. That was my survival technique. It kept me from drugs and unwanted pregnancy. It ultimately kept me from being homeless as mostly everyone in my family experienced. This was not just a lesson on fried potatoes, this was a lesson on saying no to drugs, which was one of the devils he held hands with. This was also a lesson of the paradoxical behavior of human beings. I saw the good in him as we had our bonding time, and experienced

The House that Jack Built

the bad in him as my innocence left my body. I never looked at men the same.

He had his demons to deal with. That monkey on his back, which was his drug of choice- crack, had made him so enraged one day that he jumped out the window to get his fix. My cousin locked him in the room. This was her form of rehabilitating him. But, this day he was not going to let anything stop him. It had full control over him. It reminded me of the incredible hawk. He turned into another person with greater strength. It almost seemed super human. That day he had no self preservation, or was that his way of persevering himself? He needed it. It almost looks like he would die without. That day he assessed the situation and decided that the 2 story window was a good choice. But, that is not all that I remember from him. This was no T.V show with one dimensional characters. He was not the crack addict that you saw on New Jack City. Although, I can imagine that is a fitting description of some, however not of him. I have seen many sides of him. I saw him being kind and generous by running errands for my grandmother, I saw him making himself helpful to others by helping my grandmother with the groceries. I saw him eat and drink and shop for clothes. I saw him kiss his mother on her forehead. I saw him cry and laugh. He was not a victim, no. He made his own decisions. At a tender age I saw his brokenness nevertheless, and the brokenness of this broken world which I would not have articulated as clearly as I can now. Now, his addiction started before the Just Say No to Drugs campaign. His addiction took place before we were educated on the effects of drugs and before we saw the outcome of crack. There were no movies like New Jack City at the time of his addiction. Pookie was not a recognizable character that was lived out on the movies screen at the

The House that Jack Built

time of his addiction. I saw this man as he struggled with his sexuality. I don't know if this was a calling or fate that he did not care to acknowledge, or the running from not so present let down of father figures that left his life. What I remember was that he was not one dimensional, that his wounds ran deep, and he could not be trusted.

The House that Jack Built

Grandpa Jack was a vague image to me. I don't have a lot of memories of him. I do remember that he was blind. One memory that I have is when I was young and we were in the kitchen. He was sitting in one of the old oak wooden chairs bouncing me up and down on his knee while singing to me. I don't remember the song, but I remember being extremely amused at this game. Although, he was blind I was far too young to understand what that fully meant. Blind.
However, he did most of the things that those that could see did. I remember later in life my uncles telling me all the things that he did when he had sight. They told me that he had a cleaning job. It was his responsibility to clean the local parks. He also did other side jobs, like hacking. For those that don't know a hack man is a person that drives people around for money, something like an Uber, but more of an independent entrepreneur and less legal.

There was another memory that is implanted in my head as a young child of him as well. I remember when he and my great great- grandmother were fist fighting. Yes, my grandmother, his mother in law, fighting. The fight took place up stairs, but I remember both of them falling down the steps and then got back up and kept fighting. I was amazed at the strength of these older adults. The interesting thing is although my great great-grandmother was older, smaller in size, and a woman, I don't remember her losing the fight. But grandpa held his ground as well.

Fights were a common occurrence in my family. Anytime when there are over 10 people living in a household, there are going to be fights. Well maybe not like the one I described, but you have to admit in the most peaceful household with too many people, people living on top of

The House that Jack Built

each other- usually causes fights. Maybe not fist fights- well maybe not adults- well maybe not men fighting women.

My grandfather's legacy was more than the normality of fist fights and men and women fighting. Each of us played a part in the stage that my grandfather set for his household. Generation after generation. Before I was even considered, I heard of grandpa holding an after hours spot for "gentlemen" in the neighborhood. I believe down south they called this a "speakeasy". This is where men would be able to party, gamble, and drink until their hearts were content. My grandpa thought of this as a way to earn extra money and afford that house on the "hill". The house that on paper was a social economic upgrade but behind closed doors, reap of depravity and deplorable acts. If these walls could talk I bet it would start with a weeping cry. Furthermore, my grandfather used my mother's mother to entertain the men that decided to relax in the luxury of that house on the hill. So his daughter would sing, serve, and offer conversation to the men that made their way to our home. Nothing sexual, but nevertheless "entertainment". And that was the same "entrepreneurial spirit" that ran in our family in generations after. Find women, use them, brainwash them, exploit them, and use them for financial gain. This in turn became the family business for years to come. Even women were making profits off this family business. Grandpa set the stage. This was the house that he built, and the same theme carried through many generations.

The House that Jack Built

I remember our house smelling like kerosene and old carpet, even though I could never smell it. Until one day it was bought to my attention. My childhood best friend Carry brought this to my attention. She brought a lot to my attention, and I listened. Later in life I bought things about her family to her attention. Our friendship could not withstand that. I remember Carry would come to our house after school. Ironically, I was the one responsible for watching her. Her mom paid me 5 dollars a week in order to "watch her". She was a year younger than me, so I was getting 5 dollars to play with my best friend and she was getting a really cheap babysitter. I wonder if the more sophisticated adults caught on to this. My innocent child-like mind did not think of this even though I was slightly more mature than Carry. This is usually the unfortunate case, when children are exposed to the things that I witnessed early in life. If the adults did realize this they certainly did not mention it to me. I guess they figured one more person in the house is not going to hurt. But I learned from our relationship. She taught me that everyone's normal is not the same, and some normal should never be considered normal.

Me and Carry danced to Juicy, by 357. The words "Juicy got him crazy, crazy juicy". We watched the video as these video vixens danced around in their pink patent leather jumpsuits. We often argued as to who would be the dark skin girl, and who would be the brownish color girl. We sang the song with conviction. We had no idea what juicy was, but the idea of it having a guy go crazy, we liked. We practiced our rendition of the routine in front of the big wall size mirror that covered the living room wall. We performed for who ever wanted to be our audience, which usually

The House that Jack Built

consisted of my 5 little cousins and sometimes bigger cousins. If it was not 357, it was Salt and Pepper, "Push it". Gold chains and black jumpsuits. "Push it real good". We liked the words. We liked the beat. We loved their style, we loved their portrayal of feminine power.   `

Nevertheless, with a child's mind I would categorize my childhood as fun. Despite the similarities of a depraved episode of "Everybody Hates Chris." There were tons of family members to play with all the time.   I remember coming home from school and being welcomed home with at least 5-6 children running up to me at the door and screaming my name. "Mia's is home." This was the best welcoming that a person could ask for. They were excited to see me. I was important to them, and they were important to me. We had a bond that despite the spontaneous occurrence of anything could happen at any time. Despite the incoming and outgoing of criminal behavior, we were kids, and we loved all those who were considered family. We did not even think of the psychological damage that we were haphazardly partaking of. We just wanted to play.

The House that Jack Built

One of my uncles loved to cook. He took some cooking classes in his younger years, and cooked for the army. He would make us up the best, most creative meals. Although each "household," meaning those that were considered immediate family by way of those that you depended on the most made up a household, cooked individual meals. I was able to eat in his "household." Since he had about 6 children, his food stamps afforded him with the opportunity to be creative. On special occasions he would make us homemade cakes. He would make them from scratch. On my little cousins birthday we had the luxury of having a three layered yellow cake with ice cream, although this was not a luxury to me, because my mom would send my own personal bags of food every week. Nevertheless, this was a good memory of togetherness, celebration and community. As kids we have an incredible way of looking at life. We are naturally optimistic. Those positive thinking techniques that adults have to learn often come natural to most children.

On snow days we had snowballs fights with the older cousins. The male cousins would sometimes put rocks in their snowballs to make the sting a little stronger. This is the nature of all male children. They find it amusing when people are hurt. That's why they wrestle and fight. Then they grow into adults that like boxing and hockey. This never escapes them.

In the summer we rode bikes in the graveyard- well I sat on the handlebars. I never learned how to ride a bike. Even though my mom's boyfriend at the time bought me a brand new bike for my birthday, I never touched it. The fear was too great, and my 8 year old mind did not have the wits to coach myself through the fear. One evening I left the house with my older cousin to ride his bike without telling anyone

The House that Jack Built

we left. Me sitting on the handlebars while we rode up and down the graveyard. Unfortunately, I made the mistake of not enjoying the ride, and looking straight ahead, and started looking at the ground.   I was kind of in a trance, watching the wheels move forward on the black tar and over the small rocks. Then I got scared and grabbed the brakes really, really hard. We flipped over to say the least. The whole side of my face was scarred and bloody. He hit his head on the black tar. When we arrived back home my frantic family that was worried about me cleaned my face, and then I received my first beating by my mom. My cousin headed to the hospital for stitches then received a lecture on making better decisions with Franny's daughter. That day he was not amused at his little cousin getting hurt.

My cousin was an inspiring rap star. Conventional jobs were not his thing, even though he was very talented in so many areas. Every young male wanted to be a rap star in that era. He made us this rap that we quickly memorized. I guess it was a young healthy mind that allowed us to remember a 20 bar rap. I remember it talked about us being queens and saying no to drugs. I like the idea of being considered a queen. He was a teacher, although not appointed. He was truly talented, an artist, a rapper, and a straight hustler. My mind was an open book and wanted to be discipled by him.

The House that Jack Built

On holidays we would cook this big dinner. Since there was about one household to a bedroom, one person within the household would cook a meal. This took place on Christmas, Thanksgiving, and Easter. Washing dishes after the meal was my job. My aunt taught me how to wash dishes. I thought I did a pretty good job at it. I looked forward to her approval after it was done. Her mild manner and appreciation soothed me and encouraged me. One particular Easter dinner grandma ask me to set the table for dinner. It was a long wooden antique table that fit about 6-8 people. The kids had a table of their own. This was an upgrade from when my uncles where children and they had to eat off of newspaper that laid on the floor. I begged and pleaded with everyone in the family to sit together. Each "household" to come to gather to have Easter dinner. Out of the 12 years I lived there I was successful in my task once. The amount of joy I had in my heart was immeasurable, not only did I get all the "households" to sit together and eat dinner, for that one moment in time we were a true unit. One unit. The only thing I can liken it to is the other families I saw on TV. This was a moment of value. It was the moment I become zealous for bringing people together. And at that moment in time the real pain that was flowing through each individual's heart and mind did not exist. At that time, time had suspended and we were a family. Even as an adult that has been a quest of mine that I have not been able to bury. The only way I could sum it up is when Antoine Fisher found his family. Although my family was never actually lost geographically, we were lost in oh so many other ways.

The House that Jack Built

My meek aunt was related to me through marriage. I don't know if this was an actual certified marriage or common law, which was popular back in the day. She was so meek that her eyes barely looked up at you. Even as a kid, I wanted to look directly in her eyes. I wanted to see what was beyond those pretty brown eyes. I actually caught a glimpse on occasions without her willing permission. My aunt was a short, busty chocolate girl with "good hair". I remember her always telling funny stories when we were in the kitchen together. She would laugh and it filled my soul. I think she was more entertained by the stories than I was. I was entertained by her laughter. It warmed my heart to hear her laugh. It also warmed my heart that she found an outlet to be herself.

The rumors as to the cause of the timid nature of my aunt grew throughout the household. My childish eyes were just waking up to what was taking place. There was one day that me and the kids were playing on the porch. We decided that we wanted to take the game to the parking lot that was beside the house. I remember my aunt screaming for us to come in from the porch. This is not uncommon for black families. I'm sure we all can relate to our mommas calling us from the porch. However it was rumored that she could not leave the porch. This is the same man that threw ***** out the window when he heard the "clean" revised version of my personal space violation (since he liked the second floor window so much). This reaffirmed my belief.

I soon realized that as an adult I had a need for the calmness that this lady bought to my life. Although, her being timid had landed her in the hands of people that could not show her a love that is married to respect, I watched her and she taught; sometimes with words and sometimes without.

The House that Jack Built

The House that Jack Built

My grandmother (great grandmother) was a short (even though I did not think so at the time) full figured woman. She was so adorable to me as I looked forward to seeing her smile when I got home from school. She would have me sit in a chair for hours facing another chair as my desk until I completed my homework. I remember that was the routine after I changed into my around the house clothes. Back then it was normal to have school clothes and around the house clothes. I remember my mom sending me the best of the best clothing. In the 5th grade I wore leather shirts and sweaters with abstract prints. I always had to have at least 2 pairs of gold earnings in my ear, and a pair of patent leather shoes. I remember getting so mad at my grandmother because she would not let me wear my finest clothes to school. This was right after Christmas break when all the cool kids show off their Christmas gifts. Mostly, the kids who cared about their reputation wore the clothes that they received for Christmas. My grandmother was punishing me by not allowing me to wear my outfit. I don't remember why, but I remember this punishment feeling like the end of my popularity. I went going to school feeling bare. By the end of the day, I was amazed that the situation had given me another outlook. I realized I had value without those items. As my 10 year old mind interpreted it at the time, people will like me with or without those things. It forced me to find other ways of gathering attention. I believed that I had a type of character, or swag that did that. That day I realized how my self confidence was growing.

The House that Jack Built

It seemed like I learned a lot of my childhood lessons haphazardly. There was no one known as the designated teacher. They all taught me. When my mom came by we would have our talks. She would be my favorite teacher. She did not teach so much in words but in demeanor. She was always stylish, voluptuous dark skin woman that wore her hair in a jerry curl. She always had the finest clothes and kept me the same. She had a sternness about her that I often wonder the origin.

She was respected by my older cousins. This sternness did not make her the best teacher for small children, but was very needed in my teen and young adult years. In my adult years her sternness actually saved my life. At that time, we never really talked about anything in depth, but just her presence made it meaningful. By position she was my favorite teacher. My mother was the world to me even then. All the women in my life have influenced my life. Either overtly or covertly. They all taught, and I watched.

The House that Jack Built

My younger aunt was the woman that physically disciplined me, since grandma did not have the strength to do so. I did not have many beatings, but I do remember the ones that I had quite vividly. My aunt was tall and slender. She did not look like the rest of the family. Her body was shaped like an apple, heavy upper body and slender legs. Most of the women in my family where slender up top, with real big bottoms. I heard rumors that Grandma took her in and raised her, but that she was not biologically related to the rest of us. Then I found out that she was Grandpa Jack's daughter, but not Grandma's daughter. Unfortunately, the cruelness of humanity/ family members felt the need to bring this to her attention whenever they did not like something she did. The ole I got something on you. How cruel.

One of the worst parts of living there was going to the store five times a day. Sometimes it was fun if I could round me up a walking partner. Other times it was annoying. I did not mention my frustration to my mother; however I am sure she would have put an end to it. I just remained silently annoyed.

The House that Jack Built

I remember mom giving my grandmother money and food for me for the week. Grandma kept most of the food upstairs in her freezer. I also remember a dog chain with a padlock being on the refrigerator downstairs. Grandma did not want anyone stealing food at night. After people got drugs in their system they usually wanted to snack. However, after the kitchen was cleaned and before we went upstairs for the night that padlock went on the refrigerator like clockwork. On occasions my boxed snacks from upstairs would disappear. At that time grandma did not have the energy to find the culprits. My mom would get really mad about this, but they continued to do business the way that they have always done.

Me and Carry would run upstairs after school and eat our candy we got from the corner store. We would eat it in the bathroom (how unhygienic) because we did not want to share it with the 10 people that would have begged for, as well as fought for our snacks. Grandma would make me share whenever I came in the house if it was something that everybody else wanted.

The House that Jack Built

Because the culture of our lives was embedded with anything can happen at anytime occurrence, I remember when my uncle faked his own death. We were all sitting on the porch that summer night. A phone called come in from one of my uncle's friends. He said that my uncle died in a car accident. All of us begin to weep. After about half an hour of crying my uncle walks up on the porch and said "What are ya'll crying for." Though I was a fast processor, I really did not know how to process this. Looking back it was defiantly a cry for help. That desire to be loved will make you do some weird things. I know he always felt like Grandma Mary did not love him. He was convinced that she was only taking care of him, his brother, and my mother for the welfare checks they received when they were younger. This might have been true, but I do know that grandma stopped him from making one of the worst mistakes of his life. His friends had plans to rob a bank and he was set to go with them. To return drug dealers loyalty you really can't tell them no after they have been feeding you and clothing you throughout your life. That night however, grandma said he could not go out and she was adamant about it. His friends are now serving 120 years.

The House that Jack Built

When I grew older I heard stories of my mother's'
childhood. My mother doesn't speak much of her childhood
so I would hear it from my uncles. Although my uncles
would talk from different perspectives, these perspectives
just speak to the difference in them, different men that they
have become, and also the different treatment that they
received. One sheltered, and one that was basically thrown
to the streets and raised by drug dealers. One raised by
neglect and one raised by negligence. A blind eye and
incompetent care. Both of my uncles would agree on this,
however they would talk about how grandma would give
them powdered milk and powdered eggs for 2 meals a day.
I know on some occasions they would have oatmeal and
grits because of my mom's aversion to grits. She hates the
black specks in them. To this day my mom does not eat
oatmeal because she had it so much when she was younger.
Grandma (Great Grandma who I refer to as Grandma) gave
them this meal because it stuck to the bones and to be cost
conscious. The grits- well let just say that my mom
developed a phobia behind it. To this day whenever she
cooks grits she picks out all of the black kernels. A tedious
task as you can imagine. But after the batch of grits at 1803,
this over 50 year phobia is well within reason.

My uncle does a funny skit about when he went to school
and got called into the nurse's office. He was so skinny that
the nurse would give him 2 pints of milk to drink. Real milk
was a luxury to him. Then he would end his act saying,
"they give us milk, they should have put us in a home". I
have learned how to hear each of my loved ones cry. This
was his well disguised cry in the form of a joke that pleases
the crowd, and helps heal his soul. The ironic thing is that all
the adults were overweight. I remember images of
grandma-Mary in the kitchen cooking eggs and rice with

The House that Jack Built

peppers. I always wanted to taste this foreign dish that left a wonderful aroma throughout the house, but then I would find out that it was restricted to grownups. I soon learned the sound of my own cry- silence.

Years later my cousin and I traded stories about growing up. Her stories had me beat by all means.   She talked about how she lived in abandoned buildings with her mother and grandma- Joanne (my mom's mother). She even told me that it was so bad that she would collect the cans off the street to recycle, so that they can have enough money to pay for a bag of chicken legs. I instantly felt financially privileged.

The House that Jack Built

The older I grew the more I wondered about what my mother experienced at 1803. My mother's cry sounded slightly different than silence. Hers was a tone of ignoring. "I just ain't going to worry about it. Don't talk about it;" She would say, "Why dwell on it". "It happened, let's move on. No need to talk about life as long as you are living it". I actually always wondered what happened to her. I wonder how it felt to have no parent checking in on you, and left you with guardians that either did not truly wish you well, or was not capable of doing so. However, this has always been my mom's way of dealing with pain. No use of crying over the past was the way she moved through life. She also demonstrated this philosophy. I have been on this earth for 40 years, and I think I saw my mom cry twice. When I was hospitalized, and when I shaved all of my hair off. I often wonder if she had any opportunity to process her feelings. I often thought that maybe she felt like she was not allowed. That she had too many burdens to bare, too many people to take care of, everyone's hand in her pocket, because she is the one that got a job and managed to maintain it. She was the one to get out.

I would categorize my mother as strong and resilient. My mom is the most resilient person that I know. This resilience became a must needed lesson that I had to learn from when I needed it the most. She was, and is still my favorite teacher. I formed my teachers as some young women and men form their friends. I watched them carefully and then I would engage them. I had a teacher for whatever I wanted to learn. God provided me with a teacher for anything that I needed to learn. The teachers came and went. Some stayed for a while. Nevertheless, I did not feel a lack.

The House that Jack Built

Nikki Giovanni said, that there is strength in your tears. The side my mother often showed was her form of strength. This left an unbalanced image of her. As my teacher, I too adopted this cry partly. We all process what happens in our lives differently. We all process pain differently. Some healthy, some unhealthy, some effective and some ineffective. Her way was to not cry over the past. I am not here to judge anyone's cry, but what I learned from her is, somewhere down the road of life it taught me, you better cry. What my mom taught me was that at the end of that journey, at some point you have to get up.

She later married a man that understood her cry. I approved of him shortly after I realized his eyes did not linger on me longer than what was appropriate. He built our trust. He became a strong provider. Just the average blue collar man that is trying to do his best to do right by people and his family. He prayed before every meal and tried to be generous to those who were less fortunate. Me and my step brother was usually the recipients of this. Eventually they built, and memories of the past seemed to fade. We began to build a tradition of family dinners and game nights. I started to feel at home. This became my Antoine Fisher feast.

The House that Jack Built

The frailty of an 18 year old mind that had lived in abuse that is too painful to speak of; The frailty of a woman that was never given adequate provisions from her parents. Actually had parents that made a verbal declaration by way of word and deed that they have no interest in your well being. I know her pain runs deep. I can only imagine her confusion. After bouncing back and forth between 1803, living with others, and her own apartment, I understand that she did not know her options. She felt like she had no options. She in some way was offering me stability. This taught me that no one is one dimensional and context is everything. I warned you these are not one dimensional characters. This is not what you see on t.v, this was not a poorly written script. These are real people making real costly mistakes and I share in her humanity. My cry consisted of loving the wrong men or offering unconditional love to men who did not deserve it.

The House that Jack Built

As soon as my mother could work she left 1803. She told me how they offered her to go to school or a job. She quickly responded by getting a job. My mother has never been without a job since getting her first job. My mother only had two jobs in her entire life. Therefore, taking care her brothers and cousins were a given. This meant taking care when she could of her brothers by way of clothing, food, and sometimes shelter. Even when it interfered with her peace, even when it brought unwanted activity in her home. This was the sweetness of my mother. The way she loved - Provider.

The House that Jack Built

When I was little I heard stories of my grandmother- My mother's mom (grandma Joanne). She lived in New York for most of her life. The most memorable story was hearing about her attempting to jump out a six story window of her New York apartment. Although, I did not understand fully at the time, my young mind processed the event in many different ways. The question in my mind that I could not reconcile "why would someone want to jump out of a window"? Her spirit paid me a visit on my 30th birthday, although it was a delayed onset according to the Psychiatrist. Just when I thought I made it out of my childhood unscarred.

The House that Jack Built

As a small child I remember wanting more than what was presented to me. I kind of felt like I wanted more than our socio-economic/poor, morally confused, and dysfunctional minds that were surrounding. I soon realized that you would have to leave the planet to escape feeble minds. I also soon realized that after habits formed they are not easily broken. Ironically, growing up with broken people and when their brokenness was so obvious to the onlooker. It was not clothed neatly in professional attire. It was raw and in your face. Drugs being transported in and out of the kitchen window. People gathered to do drugs often after a card game of spades, while the onlookers of children were often left to their own devices. One important lesson that I carried with me from childhood, well two, to always understand people in their context. Right and wrong does not dissipate but complexity of human beings being a consumption of experiences and desires, and mindsets and the quest for liberation, or for some to gently ease the pain for today, it is important to be aware of. I wonder what made them tick. I become insane in the quest to find what made me tick. We are complex in every way. This lends to empathy, smart conscious empathy, but nevertheless empathy.

After the assumption that I have made it out of my childhood unscarred, with hope and self esteem in tack, and

The House that Jack Built

with a desire to change the narrative, I soon realized that it was much harder than I thought. I heard it was once said that it is easier to raise healthy children than to repair broken ones. Even though I would not agree to this because my mind will not allow by way of the testimony of my own life, and the fundamental belief that anybody can change. I would say that it is hard. I also soon realized to my surprise we all, well at least most of us, were fighting the same fight to change the narrative.

Approximately 1 in 5 youth aged 13–18 (21.4%) experiences a severe mental disorder at some point during their life. For children aged 8–15, the estimate is 13%. (https://www.nami.org/Learn-More/Mental-Health-By-the-Numbers, Retrieved on Jan. 8, 2018)

CHAPTER TWO

Emergence

When I was in private school, my mom scraped every penny together from her cashier job to have me in during my early years of schooling. (The payments were so high I shortly went to public school, Elwood, Wagner, and King) I remember hearing all the children talking during class at the same time. This talking was unusual because it was an excessive amount of noise. I remember the chatter being so excessive that I could not take it anymore and I blurted out a big, loud scream. Ironically, the teacher took my side, and said you see, there is too much noise in here. Although, this was truly eccentric behavior, the teacher took my side. Her response is the only way I was assured that those were not internal voices.

The House that Jack Built

My cousin and I traveled to West Philly often because that is where she grew up. We caught the Broad street train, and the El train at City Hall. I hated traveling with her because I always feared a train crash. The loud noise and the swivel of the train kept me in a panic anticipation. We were on the orange line sitting in those orange and tan seats. I remember there were two girls sitting across from us giggling and laughing. How intrigued I was in their conversation. I could not quite hear, but I heard them slightly, putting bits and pieces of their conversation together. My eyes did not leave their conversation, only the times when I thought they noticed me looking. Well, eventually I heard one of them say "She thinks I am talking about her, " I tried not to be obvious, not wanting my cousin or those strangers know. At first I thought this was just the common suspicion that we as teenagers and young adults have. Little did I know that it was something that was laying dormant in me, asking for the right time to come out. With the appropriate amount of stress or just the natural evolution of biology, it was going to show its ugly head. It was only a matter of time.

The House that Jack Built

The House that Jack Built

The House that Jack Built

All black people have a church story, especially in Philly, where there is a church on every corner. You either have, or will have your own personal "Church" story. I remember a friend telling me that spirituality is Black people's gift. This can be dated back to Africa. Each race has its own distinct gift and spirituality was ours. Based on modern society I am not sure how true that is. However my encounter shaped the rest of my life and set me on an unexpected course.

Somehow I found my way to a church. Prior to this discovery I did not know what a church was. Well, I

The House that Jack Built

remember my grandmother taking me to the hall, but this was slightly different. It was more energy. What was familiar was that there was pretty much the same type of people that circumferenced the building. I saw all the polite, well mannered people gather in their well groomed clothes that took on the professions of lawyers, doctors, and business owners. What was interesting about them is that they were intrigued by an idea of God. I know religion has played a role in my family and society prior, I guess I just was not paying attention before this time in my life. I know that my uncle turned Jehovahs witness after he had a hit out on his life due to drug money. I know my grandmother would go to the hall and watch the Clark sisters on T.V. For the most part, I did not know much about this gathering of people. I do remember wanting to learn more because of what they were talking about. It opened the dialogue of a higher power. This was a dialogue that I had been waiting for.

My first time attending a Sunday service my ignorance to Christianity was displayed. I proudly brought my Jehovahs witness bible to an Evangelical Christian church. I found it interesting that I could not find the pages that they were speaking of. One of the older men there tried to help me because of the confused look on my face. When he saw the bible that I had, he said in a deep voice, "sis you got the wrong bible", later someone gifted me a bible.

The preacher talked of everyone one being a sinner. I had already checked that off my list. Living as long as I have, and

The House that Jack Built

seeing what I have seen, and doing what I have done, I did not need much convincing of the doctrine.

Later I grew in the bible knowledge, reading it every day. Memorizing scripture, and coming to church on Sundays, Tuesdays, and sometimes Wednesdays. That was what all the "serious" church people did. I was embedded in its culture and engulfed in bible verses. I had a reference for everything. Quickly, in my daily conversations I had a bible reference that related. So much so that some of my family members where getting a little bit sick of me.

I latched on to every word. Every Sunday I felt God speaking to me. Not audio, but through these men. Little did I know that gradually the suppressed illness that was making a way to the forefront. Mixed with Ideologies about God, grandiose thoughts about Him that I was never exposed to, and the guilt of my sinfulness weighed on my psyche. My guilt crippled me. If I took a pen without asking, or by mistake, I felt guilty. If I jaywalked I felt guilty. If I drove over the speed limit I felt an excessive sense of guilt. The stress of it all weighed heavily on mind, I am sure that my brain chemistry was being changed by the load of self-imposed stress to keep up with the rules of God, or as evangelical Christian would say, the Law of God.

The House that Jack Built

My introduction to a formal higher power had opened up the floodgates of what was already in me. In search of that higher power, the genes that flowed through me with the heavy load of stress of living began my first serious encounters with my mental break of this world for another one.   It turned out that I did not escape my childhood unscarred. Biology and suppressed issues were a few of the many catalysts that sprung my psychological break. It appeared that I could not run fast enough from Jack's house.

The House that Jack Built

I remember the story behind my grandmother being institutionalized in Upstate New York. She told the doctors that she was running from the Devil.

The House that Jack Built

Predominantly everyone my age was college grads and worked as professionals in the career world. Most people naturally where divided up between social classes. I soon realized a different kind of dysfunction. It was one that dressed in nice clothes and spoke polite language to your face, but would laugh at you behind your back, or cast down their nose at you because you did not go to a good school or speak proper English. These judgments did not lean itself to context of a person or a humble acknowledgement of the Grace that fostered these different walks of life. This would soon prepare me to navigate through corporate America. But then, it was those who would answer your phone call at 5 in the morning because you are having an anxiety attack, or would pray with you until you come out of your depression. Again, welcome to the paradoxical behavior of human beings.

The House that Jack Built

My mind started to make many associations even in mid conversation. These associations were very loose, and looking back where vaguely related. God started to speak to me much more, with impressions. I had a sense that he wanted to say something to me. I started to act in accordance with these impressions, no matter how weird and out of place they were. The thoughts kept coming at rapid speeds. They continuously increased. I would liken it to rewinding a movie and you get to see all the parts play back at a fast steady speed, but just enough that you get the scene. I lived in the book of revelations. Soon, I was not able to tell the difference between today, biblical times, and revelations. My mind seamlessly went in and out.

One particular day after 2 hours of studying revelations, I started talking to a Christian friend. He mentioned he fell off a white horse. All I heard was white horse. I remember in revelations they spoke of the white horse. I wondered if what he was saying had a special meaning. He assured me that it did not, as I was quite transparent in what I was thinking with him. Consequently, I relied heavily on the senses to interrupt my environment. Through my sight, I took a look around and saw skeletons. Everyone was wearing clothing with skeletons on them, although this was a popular clothing item, I tried to understand the meanings. It scared the hell out of me. Everywhere I saw skeletons, even on baby clothes. Now why would anyone put skeletons on little girl clothing? It had to have a deeper meaning. Quickly, I made occasions to Satan. Again, uncontrollable loose bible references.

The House that Jack Built

With all this revelations talk, I thought that maybe God wanted me to warn people of the coming judgment. I began to invite everyone I knew to church. After church I would grab a handful of tracts and stand on the corner of the block handing them out. The strange look of this seemly sane stylish young woman standing on the corner of a Mt Airy block, talking about "The kingdom of heaven is at hand, Repent." I don't know if the strange look was because they expected it to come from a different package, or if they were scared to death.

My step father started noticing my eccentric behaviors. I started looking out the window every 5 minutes after I was convinced that I saw a yellow car following me. I remember the yellow car that I saw everywhere I went. It was a little yellow hatchback car. Almost like a clown car, but I remember it looking out of place with its surroundings. It's not often you see a yellow car. My step father watched my behavior. I'm sure he was thrown off and confused because I had not exhibited to him forms of paranoia before. He also never came in direct contact with a person that had. At the time I did not notice him watching. These ideas were as real to me as the floor is beneath my feet. Continuously, I noticed a series of events and heard conversations that had a deeper meaning. I have always known that I looked at the world slightly different than my peers, but those subtle differences became big gaps. Is this God talking to me? Am I getting insight that others are not privy to know? If God is speaking to me, He was calling to me to something, was my thought.

The House that Jack Built

I saw a homeless, insane man in the middle of the street, bloody with ripped clothing screaming at the top of his lungs, although words were not coming out. He looked disheveled. He looked like he was carrying a heavy load that turned to rage. In retrospect maybe this was my rage. Or maybe this was God's rage I thought that it must have been a painful weight to bare. I prayed for his rage to turn to calm.

As I walked the streets I saw people that looked fragile and in need of help. They walked up to me asking for change. No one looked "normal", everyone looked in pain or deprived of a necessity in some form or another.

The House that Jack Built

My devotionals consisted of reading revelations more and more.   As I read revelations the pastor explained the end times were here. Even when I turned on the radio there was a pastor referencing the end times. Actually, one minster claimed he knew the time and date of the rapture. He had a huge following. People selling all their possessions.   Each Sunday my beliefs where being confirmed, although they did not mention sell all your possessions, the urgency of the end times was consistently talked about.   Each time I looked at the environment I saw an increase in violence, each time I noticed more and more the dissension in the church. Slight changes began to be noticed by my congregation. If it was not my excessive guilt for inconsequential things, it was my passing of notes that had special messages in them.

The House that Jack Built

That night, I begged my mom and dad to sleep on their floor. "Someone is following me". I was reluctant to be close to windows convinced that a sniper would shoot me through the window.   Confused, they had never been faced with a psychotic break with anyone, let alone their child. They obliged my request but watching me closely. I did not make it through the night. I felt the threat on my life was even more real.   Those that were following me and had plans to hurt me and my family were approaching. There was a rubbing alcohol bottle on my mother's night stand. I grabbed it and put it to my mouth with a very real plan to swallow it. The idea in mind was you won't kill me before I take my own life. "I will not be anybody's prisoner". Right before I drank, I saw a bright white light that filled the dark block. I heard a helicopter. I thought to myself somebody is here to save me. I immediately calmed. No one else saw it but me. This was my first illusion. It saved my life. Something out of the movie scenes looking back. But oh so real, I guess.

My parents took me to the police station because I kept telling them that it was someone following me. The police officer saw my condition, heard my story and talked to my mom privately.   They advised her to admit me into the hospital under a 302 petition. My mother could not bring herself to do that at the time. That night I slept in my mom's bed. That morning my mother had two people from the Crisis Unit that were going to escort me to the Germantown

The House that Jack Built

Crisis Unit. . Since I evaluated everyone and everything in terms of God- good and from the Devil- bad, I looked in their eyes and determined that I was not going to go with them. Later the police came to our home. I had no choice but to leave with them. I did not fight. It was my first time in the back of a police car. A little sanity crept in. The thoughts to myself "all my life I stayed out of this situation but I ended up here". I felt like I did something wrong. This was a traumatic experience for me. Hell, I am still scared of police officers today but for many other reasons. I kept looking at my pastor's calm eyes and my mother's frantic eyes. At that point I slightly trusted that they made the right decision. I trusted that maybe they were right and I was wrong.

One of the hardest things to do is to convince someone to get help who believes that they are fine, that they are right, and the world is wrong. I have always relied on my insight. That is one reason it took my friends and family so long to recognize the warning signs. They trusted my insight heavily. At that moment my insight, my judgment, my interpretation of reality was obstructed. Be assured that when one is under delusion and is truly having a psychotic breakdown, they really and sincerely believe that their ideas are accurate. This is what keeps them from getting help. In a psychotic state, your mind is the wound. It is where the hurts is, although there is no physical pain. The acknowledgments of that lead to my mental health recovery.

The House that Jack Built

The House that Jack Built

She had a lifetime of fighting for her sanity, but that is not all she was. She was a smart, resourceful person that knew her way around the system. She knew any hook up imaginable. She was a mother to many in her place of dwelling, the Bronx projects (although my mother and her brothers escaped that luxury). She smoked cigarettes and always managed to look sophisticated when doing so. She had a seductive way about her which is evident of her many male companions-her cry. She was more than her mental health challenges. She was a mixture of dysfunction and lovability. This is a plight that I would soon have to endure myself. Who I am I after my mental health diagnosis?

CHAPTER THREE

Surviving a Mental Health Diagnosis

I walked into the office and they immediately started their paperwork. I felt like I was in court and everything I said was going to be used against me in the court of law. This added to my paranoia and feeling unsafe. As they asked questions, I felt more interrogated, like I did something wrong. Looking back at my schooling, I know that they were trying to do their job, and get to the true story as quickly as possible. After schooling I also understood that their job was to make the story as juicy as possible for the petition to go through. Inadvertently, I gave them a lot of material to work with. My eyes were like I was in space. I remember I could feel my eyes hurting because they were so bulged out of my head. I used my eyes to interpret reality, which caused a strain on my eyes. Eventually after I became more comfortable and I later confessed to my eyes hurting me. They took one look at me and immediately took me in. I did not want to stay, so I tried my best to answer the questions in the way that was pleasing to them. In the way that a

The House that Jack Built

"normal" person would.   However, among the questioning I
reminded them that Jesus was coming back. "I am glad you
are aware of your faith," I heard in the most compassionate
tone. I thought the whole place was evil. They started with
the question do you know your name. They also asked me
my address. I answered and gave them the correct spelling.
I even added an M as in Mary on the end. Then they asked
me if I knew the date. I could not remember that to save my
life. In the midst of this chaos, I had not been keeping track
of days. I didn't even know the year.   I sat in a room for
hours waiting to see a doctor.   There was a T.V in the room.
Because my mind was vacillating between the spirit of God
is gone, this place is evil, and my mom and pastor may be on
my side, I could not bring myself to sit calmly. I remember
reading once that you could speed up the coming of Christ if
you had enough faith. I thought to myself, surely He will
save me, because I don't even believe in the tangible of the
physical anymore. The thoughts were coming fast and all at
once. I wasn't given a time to think. I heard every
conversation at once. It was ringing in my ears. I remember
going in this room with nothing but chairs because it was
quiet. The windows were made of this thick material. It
almost looked like the bullet proof glass you see in the
Chinese stores. The bathroom was made of steel
everything.

There was a certain protocol to use the bathroom that they
followed carefully. I guess they did not want anyone to
commit self- harm. I thought that I was being prosecuted
for the gospel. I thought to myself that Jesus was going to

save me out of this ordeal. I believed that He could do anything, which meant that he was going to free me and that His return was soon. I thought that my mom was stopping the purpose that God had for my life. I quoted the verse to leave your father and mother for the gospel. I struggled with accepting her care against what my mind was telling me.

During the wait I saw my cousin enter into the large hospital room. She had been living between 1803 and on the corner of Broad and Allegheny. I did not know of her psychotic issues before then. I knew that she had problems with drugs. With psychological issues sometimes you don't know if it's first the chicken or the egg. A lot of people use drugs to help relieve some of the symptoms that were psychologically induced. That was the beginning to the understanding of how psychological issues ran through my family. Here you have a woman that had been living on the streets and had been a victim of a very hard life, and a woman who had a chance at a stable East Mt. airy home in her teenage/young adult's years. We shared this common thread. Cut from the same cloth, although we now lived in separate worlds. My cousin looked at me with sadness. Tears were forming in her eyes. My mind was trying to process all that was going on around me. I got distracted by a conversation that was taking place between a patient and a staff. My cousin and I did not talk much. We communicated mostly through facial expressions and eye contact. Then we got separated. Shortly after, I received a call from my mom. She heard of the trouble I was causing inside the hospital, unable to sit still for more than two minutes. With each thought I felt the need to follow it. I was petrified, sad, and confused. I remember her telling me "Don't let this break you", instantly it calmed my spirit. The doctor then called me and asked me my story. I told him what I wanted him to hear. I told him what I thought would get me out of there the fastest. I could not tell him that I thought this whole place was evil, all them were going to hell, and that the only ones that would be saved were me and my cousin, me because I was a Christian, and my cousin because she was obviously too incompetent to make a decision about Christ. So what brings you in today? My mom said I should be here. Do you think you should be here? Maybe. So what's going on? Then I spilled my guts. I could not hold it in anymore. I told him that I was going to drink a bottle of rubbing alcohol because I thought that someone was following me. That is all he needed to hear. His antennas went up. "A danger to self". He followed up by what did you do afterwards? I told him I could not come here until after talking to my pastor first. "You mean you stopped to talk to your pastor first"? Yes. Why? Because I wanted to be sure that this was not a spiritual issue first. If it was a spiritual issue, you being an unbeliever would not be able to help me. If it is what I think is going on, you all are condemned to hell. Well after hearing that ear full, he said you either 201 yourself of I am going to 302 you. I choose to 201 myself. Sanity crept in, and I was shipped to Belmont Center for Comprehensive Treatment strapped to a stretcher.

The House that Jack Built

At Belmont awaiting my bed.   It was dark outside as the ambulance transported me to the back. The room was filled with blue scrub wearing men and woman. Some people where nice, others were uninterested and did not care for those in which they were serving. It's funny but even being in my most vulnerable state I could differentiate between the two energies. At that point I was so tired that all I wanted to do is go to bed. When your mind is alert to every conversation around you it is an exhausting exercise. I remember at my arrival I was greeted by a very dark man. He almost looked burnt he was so dark. I heard that he was a Christian. We would have spiritual talks. He would talk about how people got healed and people were coming from the dead at his church. At the time I was intrigued with everything he was saying, but now I think he was pulling my leg as he found a way to entertain himself during his 11-7 shift, or he should have had a bed next to mine.   While the doctors were trying to find the right medication for me, I was fighting between two worlds, terror and calm, so much so that a couple of the workers were a little stumped as to my mood swings and briefs moments of sanity and insanity.

The House that Jack Built

Mental illness knows no color line or social economic group as I have learned from my stay at Belmont.   During calm moments I was able to meet some interesting people, people from all walks of life. Until I was convinced that Obama was the anti-Christ after someone put 666 on my door.   This sent me way back. I called my pastor and asked him what does this mean.   He also told me to stay away from the book of revelations. I started to read the psalms.

Other moments of calm, I played board games with one of the patients there. He was funny and entertained me during my stay there. I am also assured he was the one that put 666 on my door after I would not give him my phone number. My mother and cousin came to visit me every day or they rotated. They brought me food (the food is horrible there) as my appetite was starting to pick up. This was unfortunate after my recent 30 pound weight loss. I did not know I was neglecting food for so long. My mother felt that she wanted to make her presence known so I could get good treatment. People that did not have anyone to cover their affairs or have a strong support system were easier to be taken advantage of. My mind was not capable of looking after my own.

There was one woman that was going to be sent to a shelter after her discharge. Her psychological issues where too severe for her family to deal with. Her father mentioned in an exhausting tone "I just can't take it anymore". My heart went out to her. I can image how both of them must feel.

The House that Jack Built

Once medication got into my system they sent me home. I started this process walking and left unable to walk on my own. I could not think a complete thought. They assured my mother that this is what I needed to maintain my health. The doctor asked who is going to take care of her. My mom said "I will". I felt my independence leaving me.

I wish I could paint the story as she lived happily ever after, but I can't. Eventually I relapsed. I joined the many that suffer with mental illness. Although I was thinking slightly clearer, my body felt weighed down like everything was in slow motion. I could barely walk up the steps to my bedroom. My responses were delayed. I could not make a decision to save my life. Like most who suffer from mental illness I was not thoroughly convinced that I needed to be medicated. I am a person that has to be convinced to take Advil, so I really did not want to go on medication that altered my emotions and mind. Not to mention the side effects. The biggest hurdle for me was that I lost my creativity and my range of emotions. At that point I was missing even guilt, I just wanted to feel something.

The House that Jack Built

Why are you here?

I know why I am here. I could see that my thinking was off before I got here.

You are lucky to be able to say that. A lot of people aren't able to say that.

The House that Jack Built

After my 3rd admission I returned to work. This was after I sat in the welfare office with my aunt trying to get food stamps with my new identity in hand. I remember the long wait, the guard at the door, white people and black people, some rude, some well put together and composed. When she took me in the back I remember she had asked me my name. My response was so slow that my aunt had to speak for me. I could not remember my last name. A little before that I had just told my aunt that I saw Moses in Dunkin Donuts. I still can't live that one down. I remember watching the people like I was a little girl all over again. I remember studying them and analyzing them. Then she started telling me about applying for disability. I just saw my future flash in front of my eyes. I saw 1803 vividly. All my childhood memories flashed before me. To myself, I said I am going back to work through whatever means necessary. I may not remember my name, but I'm going back to work. In fact my name is work. The legacy that I have been trying to escape my whole life faced me there as she issued $79.00 of food stamps to me for the entire month. I was determined to not travel down that road.

The House that Jack Built

Two weeks later I was back at work working a 40 hour a week job.

Two months later I was in my own apartment without any assistance.

6 months later I was involved in my 3rd college for the 3rd time on fulltime status.

2 years later I had my own business.

The House that Jack Built

I shortly moved out on my own. My friend mentioned that there was an apartment available above her. I jumped on the chance to orchestrate my home the way that I saw fit. This was a freedom that I was used to after moving out of my mother's house when I turned 18. This was a long overdue experience. Although my mom is a lovely person, two women living in the same house is not good when they both are of a certain age. My mother was reluctant for me to leave, but was supportive of my independence. She has always been supportive of my independence. So I moved out on the quest to live a "normal" life, and forget about what happened in the 2 last years.

I decorated my apartment with rich African prints and art everywhere. I was glad that parts of my brain were working again. I longed for the day that I could tap into my right brain, even though some would say that the left brain was more needed at the time.

I enrolled in college again. I had many interactions with college life, many attempts to complete a degree. Surely, this would solidify that I have escaped my 1803 past, since no one had went to college and actually finished. Since I had an interest in people, I decided to obtain a degree in Human Service. This was something that came natural to me. All my life I have been engaged with a "vulnerable population", hell I am a part of that "vulnerable population" as they like to call it. I love meeting people where they are, and helping to get them to step B. Also, it was a natural transition, the next step up from my current position.

The House that Jack Built

Since I tried college for over 10 years, I was running out of financial aid. I had reached the max, (yes there is a max). I decided to give this another try. I remember completing my first paper. I had so much anxiety in the past to just complete a paper. They always had to be perfect, or else I would re-write the entire paper. I would spend hours just getting a correct perfectly constructed paragraph. This time with my new found inspiration, the welfare office, I was determined to complete what was before me. I just begin to write every thought that came out my head with no direction- just thoughts. No subject verb agreement, changing thoughts in mid sentence, but committed to finish. I kept doing this over time with each paper. Committed to put something, anything down, I got through one class at a time. At the end of my schooling I had to write a 35 page paper. Now journaling is by far my favorite pastime, and of course I write books.

The House that Jack Built

Years later after changing from a four year college to Community College of Philadelphia because I ran out of aid, and had to piece the structure of my financial aid together, I eventually finished my four year degree, with my lovely Mother, Dad, Uncle, and Cousin by my side. I had made it. After several attempts, I made it. Let me assure you that this was not an easy ride. Many tears. Many panic attacks, one almost hospitalization. Jacks legacy was moving in another direction by this simple act for some, but something that took so much out of me. I was the first college graduate out of our clan.

After my extreme obsession with reading, especially on black business ownership, I reached for another milestone in my family. I felt that this was another way to be empowered. I felt that this was another great tool to stop some of the poverty that ran in my family, and giving me the opportunity to help out more. After I graduated I have launched my own businesses that hopefully will continue in my family for years after me. I am the first business owner in my family. Slowly, I began to dream again.

The House that Jack Built

CHAPTER FOUR

The House that Jack Built

Paths are often not straight

In my 20's I got a job working in a community mental health home. I took the job to pay my bills and to transition to a full-time paying job, from a part-time cashier job that I held for 10 years. I did not have any prior experience in the field, but I remember that I always loved to help those that were outcast by society. I had embedded compassion derived from my childhood. I figured anyone that grew up in 1803 could handle something as simple as this. Plus, I had an easy way in to the job. My friend worked there, so I figured if she could do it, I could do it to. Unfortunately, I knew very little about mental health. I felt my compassion would help me navigate through the job. Well I was right, it got me in the door. My strong desire to understand how the mind works kept me there and made me good at what I do. This by far was the most humbling place I have ever experienced. I had no idea that I would be sharing in their experience years to come.

The House that Jack Built

It's been 10 years that passed from my initial interview. After I went back to work from the hospital it took some time for me to get adjusted. I was welcomed back by most with open arms, especially by the director. (after I gave a clearance from the doctor). I have worked since I have been 15. Working was something that I felt I had to do. My mother always showed me good work ethic. She has worked since she was 16 and has only missed a handful of days in her entire career. Most of the days she missed took place because I was in the hospital. My first day back, I could not remember everything that was required to do my job effectively so I relied on a pen and pad to get me through the day. I took many phone call breaks with people talking me out of my anxiety. One day started to get easier than the other. Most did not even notice.

Prior to my epiphany, as a newly diagnosed "identity", I learned quickly of my limitations. They were the strong voice of society. I lost my identity of you are insightful to your opinion is void. Less than human, it did not take long for me to internalize these messages. Depression had quickly settled in. How do you restore your life when people on the job saw you at your weakest moment, and some started to lose respect for you? Or how do you hold on to a secret that is such an intricate part of your fabric?

The House that Jack Built

If anyone was to ask me how it is to live in this body with this mind, I would tell them that it's the most difficult thing I have ever done in my life. Although, I had many successes, it is still very hard. It takes a constant self-care regime to maintain balance.   Not only do I face those internal struggles day to day, I have a society that will not let me forget.   They tell me that there is no place for me in their offices, schools and social functions. Although, many are not cruel enough to say it, symbolically it is implied on every level. This stigma alone stops many from getting help.   Like little children which are very much the mirror of today's society (or maybe it has always been), by the slight indication of a "deficiency", people are deflated of their power with the exposure of their secret (or so I thought at the time).

Ignorantly, I gave up on wanting a champion. How could anyone deal with this? Hell, I can't even deal with this. Every since I was a young girl I pictured myself in a healthy, mutually satisfied relationship. Again, escaping Jacks legacy. This dream quickly died after my diagnosis. Aware that this could have turned out way differently with the slightest change of circumstances, I lost the dream of having children because I thought of the ramifications of transferring my health issues on to them. In my mind I could not risk that chance.   1803 had me beat. I was beginning to question the quality of my life and if it was worth living at all. With the huge beware of sign, "May increase suicidal ideations", on the bottle of my medication; defeat came across from many sides.

The House that Jack Built

CHAPTER FIVE

The House that Jack Built

Thriving and Deciding Your Win

Then I went back to 1803 to visit, and I got a chance to see Jacks' house. The rundown, worn house with the roof caving in, and the brown grass that overflowed on to the concrete. I saw my uncle on the porch with my cousins. There appeared no cause for alarm. I wonder how complacency captured them. Some have never moved from that house since I was born. What was the attachment? Why was it so hard to leave and change? Why was living so hard, and why did I get a chance at a different fate? I know that I am no better than them. I know that if the circumstances were slightly different then our fate would have switched. I also know that I had a part of them that would never leave me; I did not want it too. I also know that they shaped me, they taught me. I know that I love them deeply.

Then I walked across the large street that separates Jack's house to the graveyard. His daughter, my grandmother

The House that Jack Built

and I were more alike her than I cared to recognize. Her intriguing nature; her fight against the devil. I contemplated the time when a person is born and when a person dies. That dash in between makes a world of difference. Her dash left so many scarred. Through the abuse that she received, how could she be more than what was beyond her capacity to understand. The transference of ignorance, generation by generation, the plight that she was given, they did not give her a fair chance at life. Too many issues on her shelf. I was more like her than I cared to mention. Jacks legacy penetrated through her, all the way to me. I wanted to bury Jack. I wanted to keep what he possessed dead. From that point I got up and found my way, and when I lose my way, I always go back. It was time to really do something different with this dash. It was time to change my cry of silence, like so many of the women in my family, my voice was silenced. It was time for me to speak. It was time for me to change norms. It was time to help others. It was time for me to not just live, but thrive. It was time to Do The Work.

I never realized how much my grandfather house affected me. My mother seemed to be able to move on by way of not talking about it, but I was still holding on to so much. When I left the graveyard, I was changed. Now it was truly time to do the work.

My win, I survived. Now it is time to thrive.

The House that Jack Built

I quickly learned that surviving and thriving is not the same thing. Yes surviving is needed, and I applaud anyone that has the opportunity to say that. It is beautiful words, because it a mean that you did not let the cruelty of this broken and dysfunctional world break you. Surviving means that you are doing the right things. It looks like paying your bills and going to work on time, but is it living? When I leave this earth I have one wish; that I have loved hard and left no opportunity unturned. That I have breathed in the fresh morning air that God has graced me with. That I have contributed in the generation that He has placed me in, in a honorable and respectable way, and with a variety of fun and adventure. That I have challenged the norms that were passed down to me and worked to change them. That I have helped the next generation, especially those who I shared the same DNA with. Your thriving may look different, but it is essential, you have a purpose. It is up to you to fulfill it. Go hard in this one time deal. Forever depends on it.

My mom gave me some advice that changed my life. "God is pleased with you; He just wants you to live". A huge weight left my shoulders.   I have found that the yellow brick road is the main point of the story, it's the dash.

My voice started to take shape. My cry was more distinguished; it sounded more like fighting back. I remembered that I am shaped in the image of God. I remember that I was more than a diagnosis. I was a person who has been diagnosed. In the Human Service world, language matters. Everything is governed by therapeutic language. I realized that my language was not very therapeutic. My negative self talk was ruining me emotionally, physically, and spiritually. It was an abomination to my mental health. I had to decide who I was going to believe. I stopped to process my thoughts, thankful that my thoughts have slowed down enough for me to manage them, and thanking God that I got a second chance at life.

The House that Jack Built

10 years later I never had another Mental Health Breakdown

10 years later I advanced in my career managing over 30 people and more importantly loving what I do

10 years later started two businesses, alongside working a full time job

10 years later I am enjoying quality relationships of all sorts.

10 years later became a Mental Health Activist.

10 year later heavily involved in my community

The House that Jack Built

According to Nami African Americans and Hispanic Americans each use mental health services at about one-half the rate of Caucasian Americans and Asian Americans at about one-third the rate. (https://www.nami.org/Learn-More/Mental-Health-By-the-Numbers, Retrieved on Jan. 8, 2018)

CHAPTER SIX

The House that Jack Built

Protecting your Peace

After putting one foot in front of the other and Doing the Work it was time for me to finally move forward. I have found some practices that have helped me to not only live but to live fully. This is not a complete cure for mental health issues, but after you Do the Work of revisiting your past, this will help to set you on your course to purpose. Don't get overwhelmed. Its one foot in front of the other.

Here are some practices that have helped me to stay balanced, increased my joy, improved my overall quality of life, and helped me to become a positive member of society. I hope they help you as you write down your thoughts.

The House that Jack Built

I took an inventory of my resources. In the Human Service world this is known as Strength Based Practice. Some call this a gratitude journal. I quickly realized that I had more than my blinded eyes could see. Most of us are lacking in some areas and are overly blessed in other areas. I made a note of those things that I had to help me through, and I invested in them. My mind quickly turned from lack to abundance. I believed Oprah once said, "if you don't have enough, you will never have enough". I filled myself in what I did have, and suddenly I did not even notice those things that were "lacking". This new view does not mean you have abandoned your future dreams by any means, it just means doing the things that are giving you the most return for your time and energy. This has helped me immensely in my path to Discovery. I always go back to my gratitude journal and love to see those things that I chose to invest in, grow.

From that my relationships got richer, I have embarked on many adventures, and I have acquired so much knowledge. My disposition has changed; my eyes are keen to seeing what's right about the situation and environments because my eyes are trained to see this way. This has affected my mood and perception greatly.

So start your gratitude journal: invest in those
things and watch them grow.

The House that Jack Built

I realized you have to fight back and fight to win. As my voice started to take shape, I quickly realized that there are many others like me that have a story that they were not sharing. My transparency with my illness has opened up the door for so many others to come forward, not to only share their story, but to share their story with the purpose to free someone else to get help. I never realized that there were so many people that have been hospitalized for mental health related issues.   We all have a story to tell. Even people in my family started to open up about their encounters and diagnosis. There are so many people going through life, hurting in silence.   So many people feel that no one can relate to them. My voice is to say, I can relate, no need to be embarrassed, life is hard, I know. However, you can bounce back.

Who will you fight for? Who will you give a voice to?

The House that Jack Built

What reports will you listen to? The voice inside of you that beats you down or the voice that builds you up? This is an internal voice that tells you to keep going. Just a little bit more. Everyone has it. It is not natural to give up on life. Find that internal voice and find some external voices that do the same.

The House that Jack Built

Ask yourself what voice will you believe?

The House that Jack Built

I chose self care and service. I became so free when I started to make this a practice. This is so essential to my balance and well being. I can't give anyone what I do not have within me. I schedule times to be alone with my own thoughts. I make sure that I am caring for myself when I'm feeling down. I take trips when I need to change scenery. I draw close to people that will make me laugh when I need to laugh, and I move closer to people that challenge me intellectually or spiritually, depending on my need at the time. I would love to put my cape on and save the world, but I choose to start with saving myself with the purpose that I have something to give others. I pay hyper attention to my needs. It's a balancing act. Don't choose service without filling your cup. Self-care is important to your stability. Don't feel selfish. The more you invest in you, the more you are giving others a health version of yourself. We need more of that in society.

How do you administer self-care?

What are your current needs?

How you can meet those needs?

The House that Jack Built

Different than taking an inventory of those external things that you have, what do you have inwardly? What gifts and talents should you be giving the world? What are some of the things that you are good at, or you want to develop more? How can you create more with these things? Develop your talents.

The House that Jack Built

What are some of your talents and gifts?

The House that Jack Built

Self compassion was a tremendous help for me. Dr. Kristin Neff is the creator of Self Compassion. Self compassion is basically this; realizing your humanity and not beating yourself up for your imperfections or uniqueness. Self compassion is being kind to yourself at those vulnerable times. We all have short comings. It is not saying that if you murdered somebody that you should not feel guilty. But for the majority of us, too often we beat ourselves up over things that basically show our humanity. This does not bring the change that you desire. We often believe that beating ourselves up will bring about the change. Well, it never changed me, being compassionate to myself has. (http://self-compassion.org, Retrieved on January 10, 2018)

How will you be compassionate to yourself?

The House that Jack Built

Balancing work and fun is a serious balancing act.
Companies that have high productivity rates are aware that
they can get more out their workers when their workers are
living balanced happy lives. Maybe you have to schedule
time for fun. For me, I have one day a week that I don't
have any obligations, and I do exactly what I want to do. Try
it, it will give you balance, and make you a more enjoyable
person.

How will you work fun into your day?

The House that Jack Built

Don't be self centered. How can you help others? Helping others is one of my greatest joys. I love to think about ways to help others. I think it is natural to want to give back. How will you give back? Don't think about just giving back on Martin Luther King Day, but how will you give back now.

The House that Jack Built

How will you give back this week?

The House that Jack Built

I love creating. I believe we are all mini creators. Becoming an entrepreneur was partly a financial decision, but more importantly, it allowed me to be creative. It allowed me to dream as big as I can, and manifest it in the natural. It might not be that deep for you. I can ensure you however, that you have a creative side. Tap in to it.

The House that Jack Built

How will you be creative? What will you create?

The House that Jack Built

Find inspiration daily. I love to hear stories about people overcoming challenges. I love to hear personal stories of people that had it hard, and triumphed. I'm not really a news person even though I make myself watch what is going on. It's important to be informed, but I also seek out inspiration every day, this can be a story, looking at nature, or meditating on God. This is an everyday routine. I can't survive a day without it. It is what keeps me going and it helps me relate to the universal human spirit that seeks to overcome.

The House that Jack Built

How are you seeking out inspiration?

Who or what inspires you? Find it every day!

The House that Jack Built

Challenging my mind. I sit close to people that challenge my mind. I love to be close to people that give me a fresh perspective into life or a situation. Don't stay stagnant by surrounding yourself with people that do not challenge you or think just like you. I call these echo chambers. It is a time and place to let your hair down, so don't get rid of those connections, but also surround yourself with challenging ideas and conversations.

The House that Jack Built

Who or what challenges you?

What will you do to get this need met?

The House that Jack Built

Surround yourself with positive people.   This is your life line. You are protecting you perception and attitude on life. Therefore, you need these people. I recognize when I am depleted, and then I draw close to my Positive Pushers.

Who are your Positive Pushers?

Did you find any time with them today?

The House that Jack Built

Daily affirmations. I live off of daily affirmations. I believe you can set the tone when you speak positive things over your life. It's like giving yourself a blessing. It is a wish that you are putting in the universe.

What will you affirm to yourself this week?

The House that Jack Built

Celebrate small successes. I know you may not have a
100,000.00 an hour job, but God did blessed you to move up
the career later. I count that as a step in the right direction.
Celebrating small successes will make you happier.
Progress is progress, even if you have to take a step
back every now and then. Train you mind to celebrate the
small things. No one jumps from point A to point Z. Its little
steps made in the right direction. These steps are often so
small that you barely notice them but let me assure you that
they matter.

A lot of us are judging ourselves against other people's
achievements. This will always lead you away from your
purpose. We all don't start at the same place and we are all
going to different places. I haven't saved the world by any
means, but I am going in the right direction. We all have
uniqueness about us. There is an abundance for all of us.
The universe will make room for you.

Train your mind to look at success different?

What are some successes you had today? No matter how small.

The House that Jack Built

What vision do you have for your life? Vision is very important because it is a motivator. I believe in being a purposeful human being. Don't just live a mundane life. When you have a clear goal and ultimate goal, it gives you a reason to get out the bed. Everyone needs a deeper "Why". For some of us our dreams have not come to pass and therefore we stopped dreaming. Well maybe it is time to begin a new dream. All of us have a purpose for our lives, and it is our job to figure out what it is. For some it does not have to be grand like saving the world or even saving your family, but it will definitely save you. Stop being reactive and be proactive.

The House that Jack Built

What do you want to see done in your life time? What do you want your legacy to be? What do you think is your purpose/ mission?

The House that Jack Built

Protecting your peace: Everything revolves around this. This means I need to know my triggers, and I need to know what I can and can't handle. That means that everyone does not have access to my life until I know what type of energy that they are bringing to it. If it is not feeding my soul, and if it is not a product of peace, then I am off of it immediately.

The House that Jack Built

Where is your sanctuary?

Where is a peaceful place for you?

CHAPTER SEVEN

The House that Jack Built

Good old Jack

Since Jack was the first man that I looked to for security and comfort, I believed that he had the power to make things different. Maybe I was expecting too much from him, but I believe that he could have changed the trajectory of this family future. I often wonder what made him tick. How did he end up broken? What made up his depraved way of thinking and abusive actions? For every cause there is a root. By Gods grace where Grandpa Jack left off another man picked up and finished. We are moving in another direction. The sun is shining and we are moving in another direction.

The House that Jack Built

Years later we each talked about our healing. We opened up talks of mental illness that ran so deeply through our home and impacted our lives. We spoke of the mood swings between depression and excessive spending. We spoke of thoughts that have invaded our minds- unwelcome thoughts. We spoke of the anxiety that we had when in crowded rooms. We congratulated my aunts who spoke about being over 20 years clean from drugs and were picking up their life after trauma. We found a new way to communicate. We were finding the way we loved. We are slowly but surely finding our healing. We finally made peace with Jack.

CHAPTER EIGHT

The House that Jack Built

Mental Illness in the African American Community

As African American women, we are the last ones to take care of our mental health, or to get help. We are busy taking care of the world without taking care of ourselves. It has been sent down to us by generation to generation that we should be meeting the needs of everybody else, but not taking care of our minds. Self-care has never been popular among black women, especially when it relates to the mind. It is revolutionary to think this way throughout many generations. But if we think of it, it's our mind that is the center in which everything else gets its function. We value being the strong woman, while neglecting ourselves. I'm not telling you to be a selfish, inward prick. If you read Protecting your Peace you would know that my desire is to see you cast a greater vision than your own needs. (This has a healing power to it as well) However, I am telling you to lay down the wall, and find a safe place to cry and protect your mental health like your life, and your loved ones lives depend on it- Because they does. It is ok to not have it all together. Let's stop pretending. Let's make mental health a top priority. Just as much as we give value to the physical let's give the same amount of care to the mental. In the new generation you cannot get off by saying you have baggage. Seek help and unload.

We have many men that have so much bottled up inside of them because society told them that crying is not what men do. I once heard it said, if you know a man that doesn't cry, then you know a man that is …. (You fill in the blank with the vilest act that you can think of). It's time to lay down the burden of the world, process, and have a healthy cry. I think of all that has happened to you, black man, and all that you deal with in this society. Crimes against brethren, structures of racism, and the development of your manhood with the absence of a father (in some cases, forgive me if I am perpetuating the stereotype). It's time to process and deal. Stop generational baggage. Not by stuffing, but by processing. It will make you a better man. I just wish that this was popular among people in previous generations. This would have stopped a lot of wounds that has bleed deep in my family. Men deserve self-care too.

As a whole, the African American community does not seek out professional help for mental health related issues. When I first decided to get help there were many people that said what's wrong with you, why do you want to do that? The funny thing is that, this was after I was diagnosed with a mental illness. How clearer does the writing have to be on the wall? Unfortunately, for many talking to a therapist about their problem are the last resort, until

The House that Jack Built

something happens.   This is a tool that should not be overlooked. Be resilient in finding the right one.

CHAPTER NINE

The Truth about Mental Illness

Like any ailment it should be looked at from all realms, alternative sources should be looked at closely. So why do people think reading your bible more will rid you of anxiety, depression, or bi-polar? Would you offer the same suggestion to a cancer patient? Or someone that has heart disease? Hopefully not. For me it was a combination of practices that have allowed me to maintain a rich healthy life. When I had my first breakdown, there were many people that I am sure did not know what to do or say but told me I should read my bible more, that I should repent of some unknown sin, or my favorite "she has demons". All uneducated guesses of a very serious matter. A situation in which I did not deserve. I hope we have graduated from those ideas and understand the fact that it is a chemical imbalance. Although I believe that the spiritual world and the physical world is intertwined and this book is a great testament to that, it would be the worst mistake to suggest that mental illness is one that could be tackled strictly through spiritually means. Don't try to do an exorcism on me and let's not put God in a box. It's a new generation, let's advance our thinking. By all means a divine intervention in the form of an illusion saved my life. But I praise God that he provided credible doctors that can be a part of my treatment team as well.

It is not like when my grandmother had her first breakdown. This is the era of knowledgeable professionals that understands that often the brain function of someone that is suffering from a mental illness sometimes looks different then the brain that is absent of a mental illness. More research is needed but hopefully not just the professional who is trained in the field, but the common man understands this reality. Yes trauma can induce these symptoms. I would never rule out that factor, as you can see by the reading of this book.

I would be the worst professional if I leave out the importance of medication management. This might be the path that some of you may need to take. Don't disregard this option.

There is no exact reason that one becomes mentally ill. Any credible source would agree that there is no one root cause

The House that Jack Built

to this problem. More research is needed. It is not necessary inherited. It was a combination of things for me. Late onset of mental health related issues can be induced by stress. That's why it is so important to protect your peace and find proactive ways to maintain your Mental Health.

There are many people with mental health disorders who have children that do not inherit their diagnosis. This was definitely an ignorant assumption on my part. This proves that we all have to challenge our assumptions about mental illness and mental health.

Another stigma that I wish to challenge is that a mental health disorder automatically makes you dangerous. I can speak for me, that at my most vulnerable time, I did not think of inflecting harm to others. This is not like what you see on t.v. Actually stats show those who are suffering from a severe disorder are more likely to be victims than do the victimizing. I will follow by saying it depends on the person. There are a lot of us out there that is not causing harm to society. Also lets not overlook that there are people that have not been diagnosis that are causing harm to society. So crime is not strictly a mental illness thing. I look at the people that I have encountered in my life and those who have not had a mental illness diagnosis have inflicted damage to society as well.

But I hear you, how do you reconcile all that is transpiring surrounding "troubled" people. Well first those with mental illness are not the only "troubled people. And we have a great burden to address the needs of a human being before they act out in a depraved ways to say that they are hurting.

Further I must mention that having a mental illness does not mean that you had a hard life or some childhood trauma. I will not be dishonest about the things that I have experienced to avoid the stereo type. I will however say that there are many with mental illness that have grown up in perfectly good homes and have not experienced any trauma other than the normal trials of life. This too is many others testimony and another story that needs to be told.

The House that Jack Built

To the depressed, I know your energy may seem like it's gone, don't give up. We are waiting for you to take your rightful place, in your family, in society. God has a clear purpose for you. I heard a lot of cries in my life. I have learned my own.   Seek help and find healthy ways to communicate your needs, process them, and when you feel like giving up, put your hand over your heart and know that there is a place and a purpose for you. No matter how silent it may feel. Find your cry, and then find the way you love.

As I looked at them in the grave, I realized I did not want to be like them, but I also wanted to make them proud. I felt like they would have wanted that. I believe they would have wanted me to succeed beyond them, even though they did not give me the tools to do so. I felt like if they have had their shot, maybe their legacy would have been different. It is unfortunate that they died in their pain. I don't want to die in my pain.

Why did Adam bite the apple?

The House that Jack Built

No, no.

I took my place when Sojourner asked, "Ain't I a woman?"

When Harriet freed over 300 slaves

When Maya read at the inauguration

When Pearl played "Hello dolly,"

When Michelle became First Lady

I inherited my queendom when I looked into His Word

When I looked into a mirror

When I looked into my mother's eyes, proud of my hips and thighs and all of these exaggerated lines with the ability to birth you a nation

But I never was the type to color in the lines

Optimistic enough to always see the sun rise, I walk in His light.

Not scared of its exposure, with flaws and all

With my back straight and neck tall, I surrender.

This is a wisdom of your mother's mother, meeting the needs of others

You see, this is a love that quenches anger and intuitively senses danger

What will you do with this?

The House that Jack Built

It is so much more than thighs and hips

My thoughts are mosaic and my knees are postured in prayer, reflecting the image of my heavenly creator

You will find my humility in layers grounded in the perfection on my Savior.

What would you do with this?

I shine so bright that it would take you all your life to unpack the massiveness of all that I am.

For I am a vessel used for Light

I exude positive energy, infiltrating those around me into a redemptive community.

My words are as sweet as warm pie and vanilla cream, but nourishes the soul like weeks of fasting and prayer to Elohim.

Again, I ask you, what would you do with this?

It's so much more than laying on my back doing a little twist

I mean, there is a time and place for that, I won't dismiss it

But I'm talking of leaving a legacy, that enhances humanity, with a bond that encourages our community, and ultimately giving God Glory

You see, the pain of fatherless children sang, and the women that came before me, they overcame

The House that Jack Built

And it was then that I proudly proclaimed my Father's name and focused, I became.

So I ask you, are you ready to Reign?

The House that Jack Built

The House that Jack Built

What were some of your thoughts about Mental Illness before and after reading this book?

The House that Jack Built

The House that Jack Built

The House that Jack Built

The House that Jack Built

915 483 1607

906

91429191R00090

Made in the USA
Columbia, SC
20 March 2018